Teen
FAQ
Smoking

Teen
FAQ
Smoking

Patience Coster

ARCTURUS

This edition first published in 2010 by Arcturus Publishing
Distributed by Black Rabbit Books
P.O. Box 3263
Mankato
Minnesota MN 56002

Copyright © 2010 Arcturus Publishing Limited

Printed in China

Series concept: Discovery Books Ltd.
www.discoverybooks.net
Managing editor for Discovery Books: Rachel Tisdale
Editors: Amy Bauman and Juliet Mozley
Designer: D. R. ink
Consultant: Xanthe Fry, School Counselor and Educational Consultant
Illustrator: Keith Williams
Picture researcher: Rachel Tisdale

Library of Congress Cataloging-in-Publication Data

Coster, Patience.
  Smoking / Patience Coster.
     p. cm. -- (Teen FAQ)
  Includes index.
  ISBN 978-1-84837-707-3 (library binding)
  1. Smoking--Juvenile literature. I. Title.
  HV5740.C67 2010
  613.85--dc22
                                2010012717

Picture credits
Corbis: 9 (Katja Ruge), 18 (Collection CNRI/MedNet), 28 (Patrick Sheandell O'Carroll/PhotoAlto), 32 (Edward Rozzo), 34 (Schlegelmilch), 41 (Michael Keller). Discovery Photo Library: 17, 23 (Chris Fairclough). Getty Images: 8 (Peter Poulides), 11 (James Devaney), 15 (Marissa Roth/Time Life Pictures), 22 (Barry Brecheisen), 31 (D Bryon Darby), 33 (Carsten Koall), 35 (Mario Tama). Istockphoto.com: cover, 16, 26 (Baris Simsek), 27 (Alex Brosa), 30, 36 (Beti Gorse). Science Photo Library: 21 (AJ Photo), 24 (Zephr), 40 (Jim Varney). Shutterstock: 6 (LianeM), 7 (Emin Ozkan), 12 (Yuri Arcurs), 13, 19 (Diego Cervo), 25 (Oscar C Williams), 37 (Jason Stitt), 38, 39 top, 39 bottom (Marcin Balcerzak), 42 (Monkey Business Images), 43 (Paul Paladin).

SL001461US
Supplier 03, Date 0510

Contents

1 About smoking

People have smoked tobacco since ancient times, either for enjoyment or as a way of socializing. Tobacco products are made from the dried leaves of the tobacco plant, which grows in warm parts of the world. Today, tobacco is available in a variety of forms, including cigarettes, cigars, cigarillos (small, narrow cigars), rolling tobacco (for people who want to make their own cigarettes from loose tobacco and cigarette papers), pipe tobacco, and bidis (made from tobacco rolled in a **tendu leaf**, particularly popular in parts of Asia).

Tobacco grows in warm countries. It is usually harvested by machine and then stored so that it dries out gradually. This improves the flavor.

In the developed world, cigarettes are the most commonly smoked tobacco product. The most well-known **constituents** of cigarettes are tar, a brown, sticky liquid, and nicotine, a drug. Tar builds up in the smoker's **lungs**, forming a sticky mass. Nicotine is highly addictive, which means the smoker wants to continue smoking and finds it very difficult to give up the habit.

There are more than 4,000 chemicals in cigarette smoke, many of them damaging to our bodies and known to cause cancer. As well as tar and nicotine, cigarettes contain **benzene, formaldehyde, ammonia, acetone, carbon monoxide, arsenic, hydrogen cyanide,** and **polonium 210.** A link between smoking tobacco and lung cancer was discovered in Germany in the 1920s. Now it is evident that smoking causes other forms of cancer, too.

If smoking is so dangerous, then why do people do it? One reason is that during the early stages, smoking releases **dopamine** and **endorphins** in the smoker's body. These substances are associated with feelings of pleasure and reward.

> **"What often starts out as an 'act of independence' may rapidly become an addictive dependence on tobacco. The younger people start smoking cigarettes, the more likely they are to become strongly addicted to nicotine."**
> **World Health Organization**

? WHAT IS NICOTINE?

Nicotine is an **alkaloid** found in the nightshade family of plants (Solanaceae), predominantly in tobacco and coca. It was used as an insecticide in the past, and nicotine **derivatives** continue to be widely used in this way. In low concentrations (an average cigarette yields about 1 mg of absorbed nicotine), it acts as a stimulant and is largely responsible for the addictive properties of smoking.

Roll-your-own cigarettes are popular because they are generally cheaper than the ready-made variety.

A GLAMOROUS HABIT?

Research by Dartmouth Medical School and Norris Cotton Cancer Center has shown that one-third of American teenagers start smoking because they are influenced by watching actors smoke in movies. One of the research leaders, Dr. James Sargent, said: "We found that as the amount of exposure to smoking in movies increased, the rate of smoking also increased."

"A half century of aggressive promotion and sophisticated advertising that featured alluring role models from theater, film, and sport has invested the cigarette with an enticing imagery . . . imagery which captivates and seduces a growing youngster. The youngster, indispensable for being recruited into the future army of smokers, does not start to smoke cigarettes for the nicotine, but for the false promises they hold. Hence, deceit is in a cigarette."

K. H. Ginzel, Professor of Pharmacology and Toxicology, the University of Arkansas, Arkansas

Smoking—don't start!

The best way to avoid becoming addicted to cigarettes is not to start smoking them in the first place. Children and teenagers make up the majority of new smokers. Nearly half of all smokers under the age of 30 started smoking by the age of 15. As a rule, people who have not tried smoking in their teens never come to it in their adult years. Children are also more likely to become smokers if their parents or friends smoke.

Statistics show that children whose parents smoke are twice as likely to smoke as children of nonsmokers.

Today, the dangers of tobacco and smoking cigarettes are well known. Smoking is a major risk factor for **strokes**, heart attacks, breathing problems (including emphysema), lung cancer, and cancers of the mouth, throat, and pancreas (see pages 22–23). If women smoke while they are pregnant, they run a higher risk of **miscarriage** and are in danger of harming their unborn baby in other ways. Babies of smokers are more likely to be born prematurely, have a low birth weight or succumb to **sudden infant death syndrome**.

IT HAPPENED TO ME

I smoked my first cigarette with some older friends when I was 12 years old. Since then, I've smoked more and more, and now I'm on around 20 a day. I've tried to give it up but feel unhappy and grouchy when I do. I've begun to think that smoking and thinking about cigarettes controls my life.

Alisia, 15

Some studies show that 80 percent of smokers begin before the age of 18.

2 Why do people smoke cigarettes?

Most smokers take up the habit during adolescence or in early adulthood. At this time in their lives, many young people are making new relationships and trying to fit in with what others are doing. A lot of teenagers start smoking to win group acceptance.

If your friends smoke, as a nonsmoker you may feel left out and isolated, so you may start smoking to "join in." Another reason that young people start smoking is because of the social image they want to present to others. They feel it makes them look "cool" and grown-up. After they have been smoking for a while, nicotine addiction makes them continue with the habit.

A lot of teenagers start smoking as part of a group activity.

Celebrities and smoking

A lot of us are influenced by how celebrities behave and look. Photos showing celebrities smoking can make the activity look tough and sophisticated. Celebrities who smoke are often seen as "edgy" or rebellious, and they represent a risk-taking spirit that appeals to some teenagers.

Celebrities who smoke can make it look glamorous, particularly if they are fashion models who also give the illusion that smoking helps with weight control.

HEALTH WARNING

Smoking may kill the craving for food. Teenagers tend to worry about their looks and their weight much more than people of other ages. They learn about weight-control methods mostly from their friends, so they start skipping meals and substituting them with cigarettes. However, smoking also damages a person's appearance.

Will smoking help me lose weight?

Dear Agony Aunt,
I want to become a model, but when I see pictures of professional models in magazines, they are all so much skinnier than I am. I want to lose weight, and my friend tells me to take up smoking because it is an appetite **suppressant**. I know a lot of fashion models smoke, and it doesn't look like it's done them much harm. Can't I just take up smoking and give it up when I reach the right weight?
Harper, 13

Dear Harper,
Smoking damages your taste buds, so food tastes bland, and you don't enjoy eating as much. In this way, it can help you lose weight. It also increases your heart rate, so you use more energy and burn a few more calories each day. But it is so damaging to your heart and your body generally that the disadvantages far outweigh the benefits. Nicotine has been found to suppress appetite, but in some cases it has also been observed to increase appetite. Nicotine is also highly addictive–so taking up smoking for a short while is not really an option. You might find it very difficult to give up.

"It is the children with the most desperate need to change themselves, or prop themselves up, who seem most likely to adopt a chemical support-system which may eventually destroy them."

Penelope Leach,
The Parents' A to Z

Relieving stress

Some people think smoking aids relaxation and reduces stress. But these beneficial feelings depend on the smoker continuing to smoke and therefore harming his or her health. Scientists say that the nicotine in cigarettes reduces the **withdrawal symptoms** between smoking one cigarette and the next. This means that the only way a smoker will "feel better" and "relaxed" is to continue smoking!

Mixed emotions

Being a teenager is a time when strong emotions sometimes make it hard to stay calm and focused. Teenagers may think that smoking cigarettes will make them feel at ease and more confident. Some young people take up smoking because they believe it makes them feel more secure in themselves.

Teenage years form a bridge between childhood and adulthood; many teenagers who smoke do so because it makes them feel more mature.

Teenage years are often a time of rebellion, so teens may smoke to rebel against their parents. If they ignore what their parents tell them, it makes them feel in control, more able to make independent decisions— in short, more adult.

Nicotine has also been found to activate areas of the brain involved in producing feelings of pleasure and reward.

Will smoking help me succeed in school?

Dear Agony Aunt,
I get very nervous as school exams approach. Some of my friends are smokers, and they say if I take up smoking, it will really relax me and help me concentrate. Is this true?
Malika, 16

Dear Malika,
There is evidence that nicotine can help boost memory and concentration. In fact, scientists are working on developing a nicotine pill to treat people with memory problems, such as **Alzheimer's disease.** *But taking a pill prescribed by a doctor is very different from smoking cigarettes. If you smoke, your body needs to keep its nicotine levels up. Otherwise you suffer from withdrawal symptoms, one of which is poor concentration. This means you have to keep smoking and will become physically and emotionally dependent on cigarettes. One important scientific discovery is the effect nicotine can have on the developing teenage brain. Scientists have found that it can disrupt the nerve connections and make it* harder *for teenagers to concentrate. There are plenty of better, safer ways of improving your concentration, such as eating "brain foods" like fish, removing distractions (such as the TV or stereo being on in the background), and getting enough sleep at night.*

3 Addiction

Everyone knows that smoking is harmful, but few people realize just how risky and addictive it is. Tobacco addiction starts when the smoker develops a dependence on nicotine. Once this happens, if you stop smoking cigarettes, you will experience unpleasant withdrawal symptoms because your body has to readjust to coping without the drug.

Can't I give up any time?

Dear Agony Aunt,
Since my early teens, I have been a fairly heavy smoker, but I don't feel like I'm an addict. I've heard all about the dangers of smoking, and my uncle died of lung cancer, so I know it's not a good idea. But I'm sure I can quit any time I want. Right?
Marco, 19

Dear Marco,
You may think you can give up at any time, but your addiction could be more powerful than you realize. You can become addicted to nicotine in a few days and after just a pack or two of cigarettes. Surveys have shown that one-third of smokers tend to light up their first cigarette half an hour after they wake in the morning; one smoker in 12 lights up within the first five minutes. More than half say they would find it difficult to go for a week without smoking, and three-quarters believe they would find it hard to give up altogether. Also, because you started smoking in your early teens, you run a greater risk of dying prematurely from heart disease, lung cancer, and emphysema if you continue smoking. So the best way forward is to see your doctor and ask about ways of giving up smoking completely as soon as you can.

Withdrawal symptoms

Nicotine withdrawal symptoms include irritability, nervousness, dry mouth, headaches, problems with concentration, disturbed sleep, increased appetite, and sometimes even full-blown depression. The symptoms may start within a few hours of smoking the last cigarette. This is one reason why people trying to quit smoking often quickly return to it again. Nicotine has been shown to be addictive in ways similar to drugs such as heroin, cocaine, and alcohol. Over time, smokers develop a tolerance to nicotine and can absorb higher doses without feeling ill.

HEALTH WARNING

The chances are that about one in three smokers who do not stop will eventually die because of their smoking. Some will die in their forties; others will die later. They may die 10 years or more earlier than they would have done had they died from other causes.

Smoking bans in public places such as offices, restaurants, and bars have forced smokers to take their habit outside.

Light or social smokers are relatively few among the smoking population.

What if I smoke less?

Some people believe it is less harmful to their health if they smoke fewer cigarettes, or smoke low tar, "light" or "mild" brands. It is probably true that light smokers (people smoking fewer than five cigarettes a day) are damaging their health less than moderate smokers (people smoking between 5 and 20 a day) and heavy smokers (people smoking more than 20 per day). But light smokers are relatively few in number among the smoking population generally, which suggests that people often find it difficult to limit the number of cigarettes they consume. Once a habit is established, the smoker is likely to increase the number of cigarettes they smoke. There really is no safe level of smoking. Smoking any type of tobacco products, at whatever rate, damages the human body. Smoking even a few cigarettes a day, or several cigars a week, is dangerous for your health.

The low-tar option

There is no such thing as a safe cigarette. People who switch to low-tar or light brands are likely to inhale the same amount of dangerous chemicals. They are also likely to "compensate" by smoking more, or by taking more "drags" from each cigarette. Low-tar tobacco products can inflict the same damage upon the smoker's health as high-tar cigarettes, especially if the smoker takes deeper puffs. Some people believe that switching to lighter brands will help them give up smoking, but this is not the case.

"It is extremely unlikely that a 'safe' cigarette could ever be developed. The chemicals that are formed when tobacco is burned are naturally harmful. **Filters** may stop smokers from inhaling some of the solid particles in inhaled smoke. But they do not block out the many **toxic** gases in smoke, such as hydrogen cyanide, ammonia, and carbon monoxide."

Cancer Research

United Kingdom

CUT

100s

Smoking kills

There is no such thing as a safe cigarette. Despite the stark health warnings found on cigarette packs, however, people continue to buy them in large numbers.

FAQ

4 Smoking and your health

You may eat five portions of fruit and vegetables each day and exercise regularly, but if you smoke you will undo most of the benefits of an otherwise healthy lifestyle. Research has indicated that smoking may reduce life expectancy by 10 years or more. Each time you light up, that single cigarette takes between five and twenty minutes off your life. When you smoke a cigarette, the burning tobacco produces various **toxins** (poisons). The tar from a cigarette causes cancer and clogs the lungs, nicotine increases **cholesterol** levels, and carbon monoxide reduces the amount of oxygen in the body.

HEALTH WARNING

Nicotine is a poisonous chemical. It increases the smoker's risk of developing lung cancer, **impotence**, stroke, heart attack, and circulatory diseases. It takes just 15 seconds for nicotine to reach a smoker's brain. While small amounts result in feelings of pleasure and relaxation, bigger amounts produce agitation, nausea, and dizziness. After around 40 minutes, the nicotine's pleasurable effects begin to wear off, and the smoker will soon feel the need to light up again.

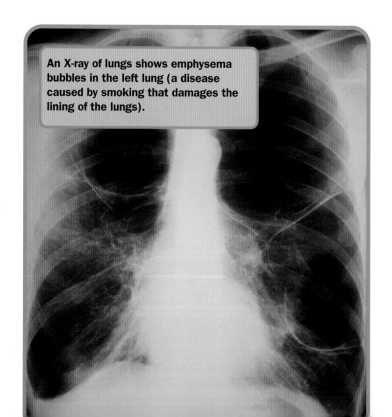

An X-ray of lungs shows emphysema bubbles in the left lung (a disease caused by smoking that damages the lining of the lungs).

Teenage smoking has been linked to depression, panic attacks, and anxiety disorders.

"Cigarette use is a powerful determinant [a factor that makes something happen] of developing high depressive symptoms . . . In fact, nondepressed teens who smoke face approximately a four times greater risk of developing depression than nonsmoking teens."

Elizabeth Goodman, M.D., Associate Professor of Pediatrics in the division of Adolescent Medicine at the Children's Hospital Medical Center of Cincinnati, Ohio

Teen smokers

Every day in the United States alone, around 3,000 young people under the age of 18 take up smoking. Teenage smokers have smaller lungs and weaker hearts than nonsmokers. They are also more likely to become ill and to use alcohol and other drugs; for example, they are 13 times more likely to use cannabis than nonsmokers. They become more tired because smoking prevents oxygen from reaching the heart, and they cough and wheeze three times more than teens who don't smoke.

Smokers as young as 18 years of age have shown evidence of developing depression and heart disease; teenage smoking has also been linked to panic attacks and anxiety disorders.

"[In a U.S. study,] about two-thirds of adolescent smokers indicated that they wanted to quit smoking, and 70 percent said that they would not have started if they could choose again."

World Health Organization

HEALTH WARNING

Emphysema is a disease caused by the chemicals in tobacco smoke, which damage the lining of the lungs. People with emphysema often get bronchitis repeatedly and suffer lung and heart failure. The gradual deterioration in a person's ability to breathe can lead to a slow and painful death.

"New research indicates premature infants whose mothers smoked during pregnancy had a higher heart rate and more trouble breathing than preemies [babies born prematurely] whose mothers didn't smoke . . . Dr. Shabih Hasan, a pediatrics professor and coauthor, said preemies whose mothers smoked would pause their breathing and be slow to recover from it to breathe normally."

CBC News report, August 2008

Lungs and breathing

When you start smoking, this irritates the **cells** lining the air tubes in the lungs, which produce a slimy substance called **mucus** as a form of protection. The buildup of mucus in the lungs makes the smoker cough. Over time, mucus can reduce the diameter of the air tubes and let less air into the lungs. This is very serious for people who already have breathing difficulties.

Tar

Tar also contributes to a smoker's cough; it builds up in the lungs like soot. If you smoke 20 cigarettes a day, you will be breathing in a full cup of tar in a year.

Carbon monoxide

Smoking also means the poisonous gas carbon monoxide enters the smoker's bloodstream. This reduces the amount of oxygen that is carried around the body, so the smoker feels breathless. It's a lot harder to breathe while exercising when you are a smoker, because smoking makes the heart and lungs function less efficiently.

COPD

Smoking is the main cause of a condition called **chronic** obstructive pulmonary disease (COPD). This describes a number of lung conditions such as chronic **bronchitis** and emphysema (see above left) that cause breathing difficulties. Symptoms include breathlessness, a chronic cough, regularly coughing up **phlegm**, wheezing, weight loss, disturbed sleep patterns, swollen ankles, and feeling tired. About one in eight people who smoke one pack of cigarettes a day will develop COPD. This rate rises to one in four among people who smoke two packs a day.

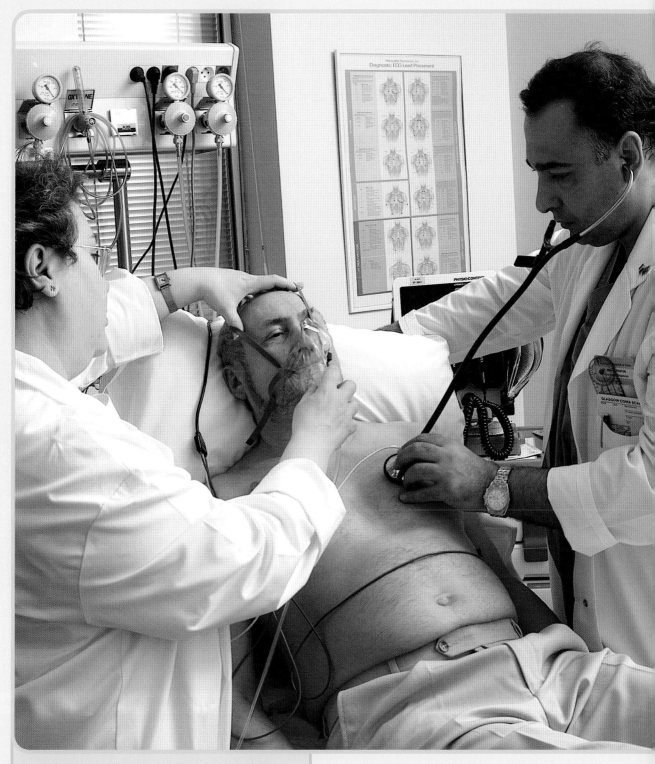

Smoking is the main cause of chronic obstructive pulmonary disease (COPD), which covers a number of lung conditions.

Lung cancer

Cancers caused by smoking include those of the lungs, mouth, and throat. In more than 80 percent of all cases, lung cancer is caused entirely by smoking. You are more likely to get lung cancer if you smoke a lot rather than a little, but it is the length of time you have been a smoker that is the most important factor. Smokers who start when they are young run a greater risk of developing lung cancer. The minute you stop smoking, your risk of lung cancer starts to go down. Most cases of mouth and throat cancer are related to tobacco and alcohol use; people who smoke and drink heavily are 15 times more likely to develop these types of cancer than people who don't.

Other cancers

Tobacco smoke is also a cause of pancreatic, kidney, bladder, and cervical cancers. Although these parts of the body do not have direct contact with tobacco smoke, tumors may form because cancer-causing substances are absorbed into the bloodstream. They are then transported to different organs in the body and destroy the cells there.

The pancreas is a gland that is part of the digestive system. Scientists believe that chemicals called nitrosamines, present in cigarette smoke, may cause pancreatic cancer. The survival rate for pancreatic cancer is low. Around 24 percent of kidney cancer cases in men and 9 percent in women are caused by smoking. Smokers are between two and five times more likely to develop bladder cancer than nonsmokers. A study in Sweden found that smoking was the second most significant environmental factor in causing cancer of the cervix in women.

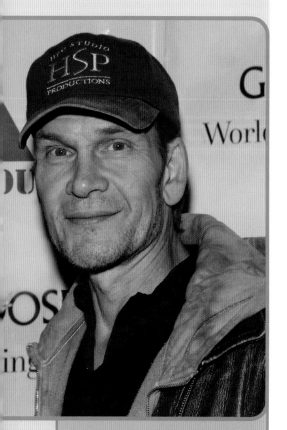

Before his death from pancreatic cancer in 2009, actor Patrick Swayze declared that his chain-smoking probably "had something to do with" the disease.

"In 2009, in the United States, about 169,000 people will die of cancer because of their use of tobacco products. This number represents at least 30 percent of all estimated cancer deaths in the United States."

Cancer Facts and Figures 2009, American Cancer Society

Some research suggests women might be more susceptible to the addictive properties of nicotine than men.

HEALTH WARNING

Cigarette smoke contains more than 80 cancer-causing substances. Scientists have discovered that these damage **DNA** and change important **genes**. This causes cancer tumors to develop because cells grow and multiply out of control.

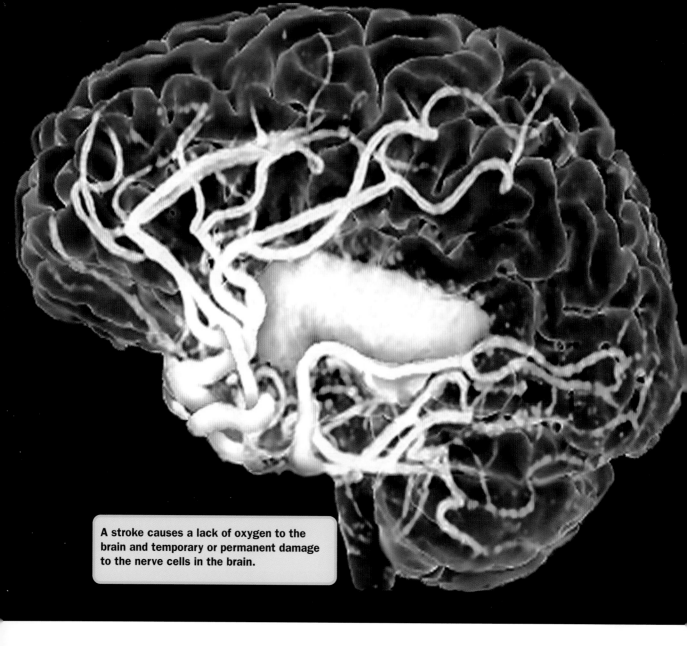

A stroke causes a lack of oxygen to the brain and temporary or permanent damage to the nerve cells in the brain.

A complex system

The human body depends on the functioning of the heart and circulatory system for survival. The heart is a hard-working organ, pumping 2,400 gallons (9,000 litres) of blood around the body each day. The intricate circulatory system is made up of around 60,000 miles (96,500 km) of blood vessels, linking all parts of the body.

Heart attack and stroke

Smoking seriously affects the complex working of this vital network. For example, smokers are almost twice as likely to have a heart attack or stroke as people who don't smoke. The nicotine in cigarettes makes your body produce **adrenaline**, which increases blood pressure and speeds up the heart. This puts a strain on your heart because it has to work harder. The carbon monoxide in smoke reduces the amount of oxygen that can get to the heart. Smoking makes the smooth lining of blood vessels rough: this leads to the buildup of **atheroma**, a fatty material that narrows and blocks them. These clogged blood vessels reduce the flow of blood to the heart and make the blood more likely to clot. All these factors can lead to heart attack and stroke. However, from the moment a person stops smoking, the risk of serious illness from heart disease and stroke starts to decline.

Smokers are almost twice as likely to have a heart attack or stroke as people who don't smoke.

IT HAPPENED TO ME

I'd just come back from a vacation in Cyprus and was feeling on top of the world. I had given all the grandchildren their presents when I suddenly felt like I was being kicked in the chest by a horse. I knew I had to get to a doctor quickly . . .

My doctor knew I was having a heart attack and called an ambulance. I was lucky that I was given lifesaving, clot-busting drugs by the paramedics on the way to the hospital. That same night I was given an angioplasty, where a sort of balloon is put into your coronary artery to open it up. Five stents (which are like a stainless steel mesh) were then inserted to hold the artery open . . .

Nobody knows what caused the attack, but my dad died of one when he was 66. Some people say it was because I smoked 20 a day for 40 years. It could have been stress—my granddaughter had been diagnosed with cancer the same year. I believe it was probably a combination of things.

Michael, 68

IT HAPPENED TO ME

I'm a fairly heavy smoker and have been for 20 years. Last year I went to see my doctor because I was beginning to have problems with my eyesight. She told me I had age-related macular degeneration (AMD), which means my sight will gradually worsen until I am blind. What shocked me was that she said it was probably as a result of smoking. Apparently the link between smoking and AMD is as strong as the link between smoking and lung cancer [see page 22]. If I had known that smoking would cause me to lose my eyesight, I would never have taken up the habit.

Sebastian, 37

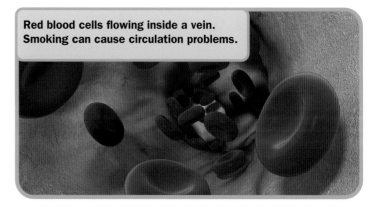

Red blood cells flowing inside a vein. Smoking can cause circulation problems.

Other health risks

Smoking affects your senses of taste and smell, making both of them less sensitive. The damage that smoking does to blood vessels in the body can result in a wide range of disorders. The reason that smokers have pale skin is because smoking narrows the body's blood vessels, making it difficult for blood to circulate. In extreme cases, the restricted flow of blood to the hands and feet can lead to **gangrene** and the **amputation** of limbs. Smoking can also lead to gum disease and eventual tooth loss, and blindness (see left).

Will smoking affect my fertility?

Dear Agony Aunt,
I started smoking when I was 14. In biology class the other day, the teacher told us that smoking can affect your fertility in later life. I always saw myself as having kids when I was older. Could my smoking habit affect that?
Valeria, 17

Dear Valeria,
Scientists have found that it is harder to become pregnant if you are a smoker than if you are a nonsmoker. Smokers are also more likely to miscarry their unborn baby. If you and your partner are planning to start a family, it's also worth knowing that male smokers have a lower sperm count and more abnormal sperm than nonsmokers. Also, it is not good for babies to live in a smoke-filled environment, so it's best that you and your partner give up the habit before starting a family.

Pregnant women who smoke run the risk of miscarrying their unborn baby.

In 1985 the term "smoker's face" was added to the medical dictionary; the definition includes wrinkles, gauntness, and grayness of skin.

Personal appearance and hygiene

As well as making skin look sallow (pale and yellowy), smoking causes skin on the face, particularly around the mouth, to wrinkle prematurely. It results in bad breath, stained teeth, smelly hair and clothes, and yellow nails. It also makes the clothes of people around you smell bad. You may not notice the smell of stale cigarettes on your hair and body—but other people will!

Hair loss

Smoking accelerates the aging process, of which hair loss is just one symptom. It is thought that smoking causes hair loss because it restricts the flow of blood to the scalp. Men who smoke 20 or more cigarettes a day have a greater chance of developing baldness. Tests on mice exposed them to cigarette smoke for three months; most of the mice developed bald patches and gray hair.

Looking and feeling older

Smoking destroys the body's cells. Breathless and tired, heavy smokers both look and feel older than their physical age. Scientists have also discovered that middle-aged people who smoke may have high blood pressure or diabetes and are far more likely to develop **dementia** in later life.

My grandad has smoked for years . . .

Dear Agony Aunt,
I smoke 10 to 20 cigarettes a day. My dad goes on at me about the dangers of smoking. My grandad is 80 and has smoked all his life. If smoking hasn't done him any harm, why should I worry?
Xavier, 15

Dear Xavier,
Your grandad may have smoked cigarettes and managed to live to a ripe old age, but he just may be lucky. Not all smokers get cancer, and some nonsmokers do get it. Some people may carry genes that make it more likely for them to develop cancer. But years of research have proved that smoking does cause cancer and that smokers are, on average, much more likely to get cancer than nonsmokers. The fact is that half of all smokers will eventually die from cancer or other smoking-related illnesses. And a quarter of smokers die in middle age, between the ages of 35 and 69. I'm afraid that your dad is right to keep after you about smoking!

IT HAPPENED TO ME

For several years, I worked in an office where people smoked all day. If I opened the windows for some air, they complained about the cold. Sitting in that environment made my eyes stream, gave me a sore throat, and made my clothes stink of smoke. I have recently had tests that reveal the early stages of lung cancer. I am devastated and believe it is the result of my having worked in a smoke-filled office. I have never been a smoker myself.

Teodora, 30

Secondhand smoke

Secondhand smoke is the smoke you can inhale from other people's cigarettes, even if you don't smoke yourself. Secondhand smoke comes from the tip of a cigarette and the smoke that is breathed back out by the smoker. Wherever people smoke, secondhand smoke is in the air. Even if you open a window, secondhand smoke will still be present in a room after two and a half hours! Although you may not be able to see or smell any smoke, it's probably still there. Smoking in a car is even worse because all the smoke becomes concentrated in a small space.

People who breathe secondhand smoke are at risk of the same diseases as smokers, including bronchitis and **pneumonia**. **Asthma** sufferers are at particular risk from smoking or smoke-filled environments. In the United States, secondhand smoke causes cancer and is responsible for approximately 3,000 lung cancer deaths in nonsmokers each year.

Symptoms of exposure to secondhand smoke may include irritation of the eyes, nose, and throat; coughing; and chest pain. Children and babies exposed to tobacco smoke are more likely to get ear infections and asthma.

Smoking in public places can put others at risk.

Smoking in a car means all of the smoke is concentrated into a small space.

"Secondhand smoke is an important women's issue. Women everywhere are exposed to secondhand smoke and suffer serious health consequences because of it. In the Asian region where, on average, more than 60 percent of men are smokers, millions of women and children suffer from secondhand smoke. New evidence shows that parental smoking contributes to higher rates of sudden infant death syndrome as well as asthma, bronchitis, colds, and pneumonia in children."

Dr. Gro Harlem Brundtland, former World Health Organization director-general

FAQ

5 Manufacture, smuggling, and advertising

The global tobacco industry is a huge money-making operation dedicated to keeping smokers addicted. As an industry saying goes: "An addicted customer is a customer for life, no matter how short that life is." And money means power; there is evidence to suggest that some private companies funding scientific research projects can influence the outcome of the research so that it shows them in a more favorable light.

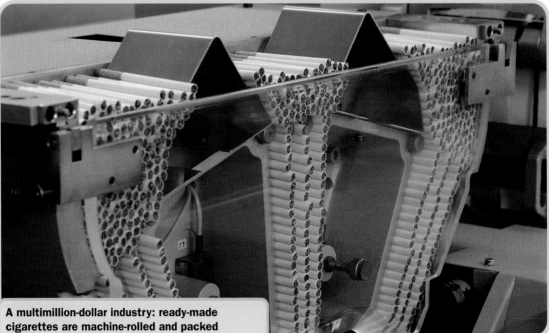

A multimillion-dollar industry: ready-made cigarettes are machine-rolled and packed for distribution and sale.

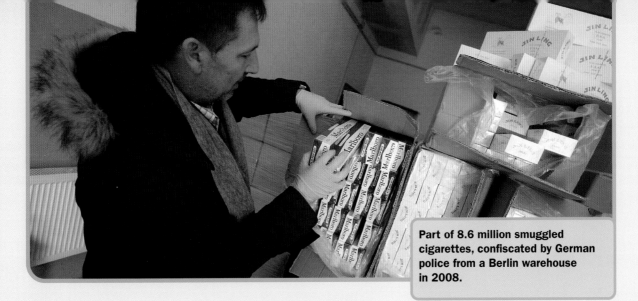

Part of 8.6 million smuggled cigarettes, confiscated by German police from a Berlin warehouse in 2008.

Tax

Governments raise tax on tobacco products, which means that they increase the sale price by a certain percentage and use this amount to finance government spending. If tax were increased, it would make tobacco more expensive, and this would encourage people to give up smoking or never take it up in the first place. Some tobacco companies lobby politicians to vote in favor of deregulating tobacco. This would involve removing tax and other controls.

Smuggling

Tobacco smuggling and the selling of tobacco at a low price on the black market means governments lose out on tax. **Organized criminals** recruit people, often girls as young as 15, to smuggle cigarettes in their luggage. Tobacco smuggling costs lives because it causes more people to smoke. Governments are unable to raise tobacco tax on the smuggled goods, and this affects their ability to encourage people not to smoke. It is estimated that about one-third of all internationally traded cigarettes are smuggled (350 billion cigarettes per year), causing billions of lost government revenue. Tobacco smuggling is an international problem that needs to be tackled at a global level.

RACKETEERING

There is evidence to suggest that some tobacco companies have organized tobacco smuggling for their own commercial interests. The companies still get paid the same, but because there is no tax, people buy more. Several major multinational tobacco companies have been subjected to inquiries and legal action for **racketeering**. As a result, the companies have begun to work more with governments to try to curb the problem.

"Cigarette smuggling is a serious organized crime and often provides the funding for much larger criminal operations such as drug smuggling or people trafficking."

A U.K. Border Agency spokesperson, quoted in the *Guardian* newspaper, September 2009

IMPERIAL TOBACCO

In 2009, Imperial Tobacco became involved in a protest over a major televised tennis event in Switzerland. While tobacco advertising has been banned in European Union (EU) states since 2005, Switzerland is not in the EU, and tobacco sponsorship is legal there. Davidoff, the main sponsor of the Basle ATP World Tour 500 tournament, is a tobacco company whose cigarette brand is owned by Imperial. The incident prompted protests from the World Health Organization and anti-tobacco campaigners.

WORLDWIDE BAN

The Federation Internationale de l'Automobile (FIA) is the governing body for world motor sport and is responsible for regulating the major international motor sport championships. In April 2002, the FIA made a decision to refuse sponsorship by the tobacco industry. It also outlined how the sport would achieve a worldwide ban by 2006. However, an outright ban on tobacco sponsorship has yet to come into effect.

Advertising and sponsorship

Advertising encourages people to buy and smoke cigarettes. The tobacco industry spends billions every year on advertising and sponsorship. Direct advertising of tobacco products is now banned in the United States, the United Kingdom, and many other countries, but the tobacco industry still gains publicity by sponsoring high-profile sports events in countries where tobacco advertising is still legal.

Display in shops

Putting tobacco out of sight in shops can help reduce cigarette smoking by young people. A survey has shown that when cigarettes are on display, one-third of teenagers think they can successfully buy cigarettes, but when tobacco products are hidden away in shops, only a quarter of the teenagers questioned believe they can buy them. However, people who believe that lower sales will harm the profits of small businesses have criticized the idea of an outright ban on displaying tobacco in shops.

The tobacco industry spends billions every year on promotion, sponsorship, and advertising.

A survey has shown that when cigarettes are on display, more teenagers are likely to buy them than when they are kept hidden from view.

"Tobacco advertising plays a key role in encouraging young people to smoke. In countries around the world, billions of dollars are being spent on sophisticated tobacco advertising and promotions, portraying tobacco use as 'fun,' 'glamorous,' 'mature,' 'modern,' and 'Western.'"

World Health Organization

FAQ

6 Quitting

To quit smoking takes determination and persistence.

Once you have decided to quit smoking, it's important to accept that it won't be easy, but it is certainly possible because people are quitting every day. Quitting takes determination and persistence—you may need to make several attempts before you succeed.

It helps to prepare yourself well in advance: decide on a day to quit and then get rid of all cigarettes the night before. Plan things to occupy yourself to avoid the cravings you will feel for the first few days. Remember: cigarette cravings last for only 3 to 5 minutes; if you can avoid smoking for that length of time, the craving will just fade away. Try putting aside the money you would have spent on cigarettes —use it to buy yourself regular treats. You could also choose to save up the money for a bigger reward like a vacation or an up-to-the-minute phone or gadget.

How long will the symptoms last?

Dear Agony Aunt,
I have just given up smoking but am feeling terrible. I have headaches all the time, and I keep getting moody with everyone. I'm also having trouble sleeping, so I feel tired and find it hard to concentrate during the day. How long will I feel like this?
Jiao, 15

Dear Jiao,
You will tend to feel worst for the first few days. You should stop feeling dizzy after about two days, but you will probably feel irritable and low for around four weeks. After that your mood should start to improve. You may feel restless for this length of time, too. After about two weeks, you will find that you are able to concentrate better. If you find yourself craving a cigarette, try the "4 Ds:"

- *delaying acting on the urge to smoke*
- *deep breathing*
- *drinking water*
- *doing something else.*

Feeling bad

Nicotine is removed from the body within two days of smoking your last cigarette. It is in these early stages that you will almost certainly feel worse. You may well suffer from withdrawal symptoms (see page 15). But it's important to remember that these unpleasant symptoms are only temporary. Try keeping a smoking diary for a week, jotting down when and where you smoke, and how you feel before and afterward. You may spot patterns and triggers that prompt you to light up. If you notice these, write down how you could deal with them if you were to give up smoking. A good way to break the smoking habit is to replace that habit with a new one, such as a sport or hobby.

Giving up smoking can make you moody and argumentative.

I want to give up, but . . .

Dear Agony Aunt,
I have been smoking cigarettes for the last couple of years. I worry about what smoking is doing to my health, but it's hard to quit.
I tried nicotine gum, but I'm not allowed to chew it in school.
Sasha, 17

Dear Sasha,
Giving up smoking can be difficult. However, there is lots of support available to you when you decide to quit. Here are some helpful tips.

- *Talk to your doctor. Doctors can offer lots of support and advice about giving up smoking.*
- *Find out about local support groups. Your doctor should be able to give you details, or check out some of the resources on page 45.*
- *Think about the treats you could buy with the money you currently spend on cigarettes—for example, new clothes, books, or CDs.*
- *Ask your family and friends to support you.*

Talk to your doctor
Your doctor will be able to offer support and advise you about medicines that you can use to help you quit, such as nicotine patches, gum, and inhalers (see page 41). He or she may also be able to provide information about support groups in your area.

A quit-smoking program can teach you techniques to use when giving up smoking.

Find out about local support groups

You may want to try a quit-smoking program or support group to help you quit. These programs can work well if you are willing to commit to them. They teach problem-solving and other coping skills. A quit-smoking program can help you quit smoking for good by:

- helping you better understand why you smoke
- teaching you how to handle withdrawal and stress
- teaching you tips to help resist the urge to smoke.

"Nicotine addiction has historically been one of the hardest addictions to break."

The American Heart Association

Your doctor will be able to offer support and advise you about medicines that can help you quit.

THE COST OF SMOKING

Smoking is not only bad for your health and your appearance; it is also very expensive. A single pack of cigarettes can cost you $8 to $9 (£5.50). The expense adds up over a lifetime. Smoking 20 cigarettes a day for 40 years could cost you more than $130,000 (£80,000)! And that's at today's prices; cigarettes will get more expensive every year.

Weight gain

Many people worry about gaining weight when they quit smoking. But not everyone does, and most gain only about 2 to 4 pounds (1 or 2 kilos). The gain is usually temporary, but, even so, it is better than carrying on smoking!

Getting help

People who try to give up smoking without any medication or support tend to be less successful than those who accept help. Support is available in many forms: local and national organizations and help hotlines offer advice; email support is available and top quitting tips can be found online; and certainly encouragement from friends and family can also be a big help.

Support to give up smoking is available in many forms.

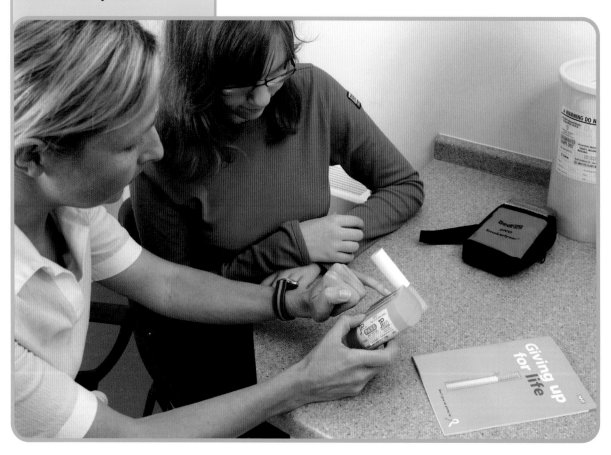

A nicotine patch provides a steady, controlled dose of nicotine throughout the day, thereby reducing the effects of nicotine withdrawal.

IT HAPPENED TO ME

I was 43 years old and had been smoking for 30 years when I suffered a stroke. After several weeks in the hospital, I began using NRT to stop the cravings for a cigarette. I've now quit completely. As a result of stopping smoking, I've saved so much money that I've redecorated my whole house so it no longer smells of smoke. Last week my doctor gave me the all-clear, so now I'm planning a long, sunny vacation.

Emilie, 46

Nicotine replacement therapy

Nicotine replacement therapy (NRT) provides your body with nicotine, but in smaller amounts than your body is used to from smoking cigarettes. NRT can help reduce withdrawal symptoms. It comes in the form of nicotine patches that you apply to your skin, chewing gum, lozenges, inhalers, and tablets. NRT products are available from pharmacies and some supermarkets. Check with a doctor or pharmacist to see if you can use NRT.

Complementary therapies

Complementary or alternative therapies for smoking addiction include **acupuncture** and **hypnotherapy**. While there is little scientific proof that these therapies work, people have successfully quit smoking by using them.

"[In Victoria, Australia] Over a fifth of smokers had used nicotine replacement therapy in their attempt to quit. Of smokers who have used nicotine replacement therapy, two-thirds use it to quit, with 17 percent using the quitting aids to cut back, and 7 percent using patches and gum to get through in situations when they can't smoke."

Quit Evaluation Studies,
Volume 10

Help a friend quit . . .

If a friend of yours wants to give up smoking, there are a number of things you can do to help. Start by offering lots of support and encouragement; try to be patient if they are bad tempered or irritable. Don't nag or make your friend feel like a failure for lapsing and having a cigarette—nagging just makes matters worse! Arrange to meet up in places where smoking is not allowed. This is becoming easier and easier, as smoking is banned in most workplaces and public places such as shopping malls, restaurants, movie theaters, concert venues, sporting events, and on public transportation. Tell your friend that he or she can access lots of outside support, too, including telephone hotlines or sessions with a counselor.

A good way to break the smoking habit is to replace it with a new habit, such as a sport or hobby.

To deal with cigarette cravings, try drinking a lot of liquids, especially water, and avoid sugary and fatty food.

Difficult situations

Even after you have quit, you will still find yourself in situations that you will associate with your former life as a smoker. Try to avoid places where lots of other people smoke or drink alcohol. If people offer you cigarettes, ask them not to. Say: "No, thanks—I'm not a smoker." Change your usual routines; for example, if you used to smoke after a meal, leave the table and find something else to do instead. If you do lapse and have a cigarette, don't feel bad about yourself and don't use it as an excuse to start smoking again. Think about why you did it and how to avoid that trigger in the future.

STOP-SMOKING GROUPS

Medical clinics often run stop-smoking groups. Although many smokers may be put off by the idea of groups, people who attend them report that they are enjoyable social occasions in which they learn a lot from one another about how to tackle problems associated with quitting smoking. People say that their resolve not to smoke is strengthened by not wanting to let the group down.

Glossary

acetone a colorless, flammable (able to catch fire) liquid used in the manufacture of chemicals and as a thinner for paints and varnishes

acupuncture a treatment for physical and psychological conditions; it involves inserting very fine needles into the body at specific points

adrenaline a hormone produced by the adrenal gland and released into the bloodstream; adrenaline raises the heart and respiratory rates, increases blood flow to the muscles, increases blood sugar, and dilates the pupils of the eye

alkaloid a substance found in plants that has a marked physiological effect on humans; alkaloids include drugs such as morphine, strychnine, and nicotine

Alzheimer's disease a terminal illness that is the most common form of dementia. It causes physical changes in the brain resulting in memory loss, confusion, and often delusions or hallucinations.

ammonia a colorless gas; a solution of ammonia can be used as a cleaning fluid

amputation the cutting off of a limb by a surgeon

arsenic a poison

asthma a condition affecting a person's airways. People with asthma wheeze, have a tight chest, and are short of breath.

atheroma a fatty deposit in an artery, which restricts the flow of blood around the body

benzene a colorless, poisonous, flammable liquid, present in petroleum

bronchitis inflammation of the airways in the lungs, resulting in coughing and breathlessness

carbon monoxide a poisonous, odorless, tasteless gas, most commonly found in the exhaust fumes from vehicles

cell the basic unit of all living things. There are millions of cells in the human body.

cholesterol a fatty substance in the human body, needed for the body to function; however, cholesterol levels that are too high can lead to strokes and heart attacks

chronic something that is long term and for which there is treatment, but no cure

constituent an element that forms part of a whole

dementia a loss of brain function and ability

derivative something that comes from another source

DNA Deoxyribonucleic acid, a substance found in cells. Its makeup is unique to each individual.

dopamine a chemical present in the brain, which enables nerve cells to communicate with one another

endorphin a substance occurring naturally in the brain that blocks pain sensation

filter the porous "plug" at the mouth end of a cigarette that absorbs some harmful substances such as tar

formaldehyde a colorless, poisonous gas

gangrene the death and decay of body tissue

gene the part of DNA that contains the pattern for every individual, influencing growth, development, and appearance

hydrogen cyanide a colorless, poisonous liquid

hypnotherapy a treatment for emotional and psychological conditions; hypnotherapy involves the use of hypnosis to treat patients

impotence the inability for a man to perform sexual intercourse

lungs the main organs of the respiratory system, enabling breathing

miscarriage the failure of a pregnancy before 24 weeks

mucus a slimy substance secreted by the body's mucus membranes

organized criminals criminal activities taking place within a centrally controlled formal structure, for example, the Mafia

phlegm mucus secreted by the walls of the respiratory tract

pneumonia a respiratory disease resulting in inflammation of the lungs and congestion

polonium 210 a radioactive, highly poisonous chemical

racketeering taking part in a racket, or criminal activity

stroke a condition that results from an interrupted blood flow, causing a lack of oxygen to the brain and temporary or permanent damage to the nerve cells in the brain

sudden infant death syndrome also known as crib death, the sudden death of a baby with no obvious cause

suppressant something that keeps another thing in check

tendu leaf the leaf of a species of tree found in Asia

toxic poisonous or harmful to living things

toxins toxic substances

withdrawal symptoms physical and emotional effects that result from stopping the use of an addictive substance

Further information

WEBSITES

www.cdc.gov/healthyyouth
The Division of Adolescent and School Health (DASH) is a division of the Centers for Disease and well-being of children and young people.

http://kidshealth.org/teen
Advice for teens on dealing with all sorts of health issues, including smoking. The site includes separate sections for teens and younger kids.

www.lungsusa.org
The website of the American Lung Association offers information for improving lung health and preventing lung disease.

http://www.teendrugabuse.us
This website features content about teen drug abuse and addiction in the United States.

http://whqlibdoc.who.int/fact_sheet/1998/FS_197_eng.pdf
A World Health Organization fact sheet listing the health risks from tobacco use.

BOOKS

Lydia D. Bjornlund, *Teen Smoking*, Reference Point Press, Inc., 2010.

David Brizer, M.D., *Quitting Smoking for Dummies*. John Wiley and Sons, 2003.

Joan Esherick, *Clearing the Haze: A Teen's Guide to Smoking-Related Health Issues*, Mason Crest Publishers, 2004.

Greenhaven Press, *Teen Smoking*, from the At Issue series, Cengage Gale, 2009.

Margaret O. Hyde, *Smoking 101: An Overview for Teens*, Lerner Publishing, 2005.

Index